Ryan
and Jimmy

To Ryan and Jimmy's parents, Mark and Susan, whose selfless efforts
in making the Ryan's Well Foundation such a success are
incalculable in value and lives saved.
To my home team, Aislinn, Ben and Joanne, who make all things right.
And to two remarkable young people, Ryan and Jimmy,
whose determined spirits allowed the unseen hand of goodness
to bring them together.

Acknowledgments

Many have played a part in making this story possible. In particular, I'd like to
mention all those people, empowered by the simple message of hope provided
by water, who have helped sustain the work of Ryan's Well. I would also like to
thank Canadian Physicians for Aid and Relief, past and current members of the
Ryan's Well Foundation board, Tom Omach, Gizaw Shibru and many, many more
people who have helped bring this story to its happy conclusion.

Photos: Cover and page 47 © Bill Grimshaw. All other photos © the Hreljac family.

First paperback edition 2008

CitizenKid™ is a trademark of Kids Can Press Ltd.

Text © 2006 Herb Shoveller
Maps © 2006 Kids Can Press

Kids Can Press acknowledges the financial support of the Government of Ontario,
through the Ontario Media Development Corporation's Ontario Book Initiative; the
Ontario Arts Council; the Canada Council for the Arts; and the Government of
Canada, through the CBF, for our publishing activity.

Published in Canada by
Kids Can Press Ltd.
25 Dockside Drive
Toronto, ON M5A 0B5

Published in the U.S. by
Kids Can Press Ltd.
2250 Military Road
Tonawanda, NY 14150

www.kidscanpress.com

Edited by Valerie Wyatt
Designed by Marie Bartholomew
Background art by Ben Lobko

The hardcover edition of this book is smyth sewn casebound.
The paperback edition of this book is limp sewn with a drawn-on cover.
Manufactured in Singapore, in 2/2013 by Tien Wah Press (Pte) Ltd.

CM 06 0 9 8 7 6 5 4
CM PA 08 0 9 8 7 6 5 4

FSC
www.fsc.org
MIX
Paper from
responsible sources
FSC® C019704

Library and Archives Canada Cataloguing in Publication

Shoveller, Herb
    Ryan and Jimmy : and the well in Africa that brought them together

Written by Herb Shoveller.

ISBN 978-1-55337-967-6 (bound) ISBN 978-1-55453-271-1 (pbk.)

1. Hreljac, Ryan—Juvenile literature. 2. Ryan's Well Foundation—
Juvenile literature. 3. Wells—Africa—Juvenile literature. 4. Caring in
children—Juvenile literature. 5. International cooperation—Juvenile
literature. I. Title.

HV28.H74S56 2006   j361.7'4'092   C2005-907886-3

Kids Can Press is a *lorus*™ Entertainment company

Ryan and Jimmy

And the Well in Africa That Brought Them Together

By Herb Shoveller

CitizenKid™

A collection of books that inform children about the world and inspire them to be better global citizens

Kids Can Press

One

Agweo village, Uganda, Africa, July 2000

Thwump, thwump, thwump ...

The slow, rhythmic beat sounded like distant thunder. It started as a dull rumble, hardly noticeable, but grew louder as the jeeps drew nearer to it. The passengers squirmed at the edges of their seats, straining to see through the thick curtain of grasses lining the dirt road.

The grass curtain gradually thinned and then opened to reveal a remarkable scene. Two lines of people stretched as far as the eye could see on either side of the road. The source of the sound soon became clear.

Not thunder claps, but villagers—adults and students and children—all clapping together. Thousands of pairs of hands clapping to welcome the jeeps.

"Reeaannn," the welcomers called out gently. "Reeaannn."

"You'd better get out, Ryan," said guide Gizaw Shibru. "They want to see you."

Nine-year-old Ryan Hreljac (*Hurl-jack*) turned to his mother. "Go on, Ryan," she said. "They want you."

This is nine-year-old Ryan Hreljac in northern Uganda, a long way from home.

Cautiously, Ryan stepped out of the vehicle into the shimmering African heat. His parents joined him, and they began the long walk down the reception line.

Ryan felt all eyes on him. To add to the pressure, a camera crew that had come with them from Canada was following his every move. They were making a TV documentary about Ryan's visit to Africa.

Thoughts and fears chased through Ryan's head. *Please don't let me mess up.* He glanced back at his father, who gave him a nod of encouragement.

"Reeeannn, Reeeaaaannn," the villagers chanted quietly. The small, skinny boy waved cautiously and shyly to the people, keeping his hand low. He was embarrassed by the attention and didn't want to look like a show-off.

Behind him, tears rolled down Susan Hreljac's cheeks. It was the kind of reception you might expect for royalty, such as a young prince, but this applause was being showered on an ordinary child—her child.

Ryan is followed by a TV film crew as he takes the long walk down the reception line.

As he walked, Ryan's eyes searched the crowd. He was trying to pick out a face he'd seen only in photographs. It was the face of Akana Jimmy (in Jimmy's part of Africa, people say their last names first).

Ryan scanned face after face, but there was no Jimmy. He had to be here. This was his home, his village. Even though there was happiness all around him, Ryan's spirits were sinking. He had hoped his pen pal would be the first to meet him.

It seemed like forever before the end of the road came in sight. Ryan could make out a large group of people milling around at a spot that looked like a small work site.

The clapping got louder … and slowly died out. And then! There, waiting for him in the crowd, was Jimmy. The two boys smiled at one another and shook hands awkwardly. There were too many people looking on to do much else.

The meeting of Ryan Hreljac and Akana Jimmy was a link in a chain of events that had started four years earlier in a classroom in a small town in Canada.

What had brought Ryan halfway around the world to meet his pen pal?

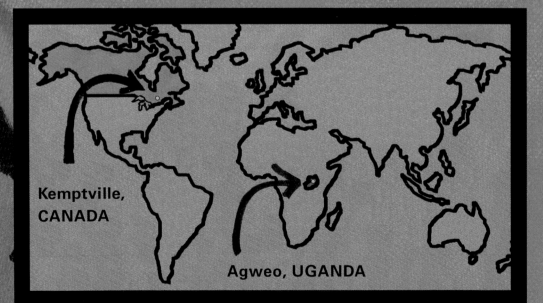

Kemptville, CANADA

Agweo, UGANDA

6

Holy Cross School, Kemptville, Ontario, 1998

It was a tough day for Grade 1 pupil Ryan Hreljac. He had just learned some upsetting news.

His teacher had been talking to the class about problems facing people in other parts of the world. One of the most serious problems, she told them, was the lack of safe drinking water. Bad water was causing thousands and thousands of people, including children, to become sick and even die.

That's crazy, Ryan thought. In his house — the home he shared with his parents, two brothers and a dog, Riley — he could use as much water as he wanted. There was water to drink, water to bathe, water to fill the swimming pool, water for the gardens — all at the turn of a tap. Now the teacher was telling him children die because they can't get safe drinking water. It was hard to believe. On top of that, she said, people had to walk as far as 20 km (12 mi.) every day in search of water. And even if they were successful, the water they found was likely to be brown and smelly and filled with stuff you couldn't even imagine, let alone drink.

It took a while for it all to sink in. The teacher told them that in Africa it cost only $70 to build a well that could supply a village and surrounding area with safe, clean water.

Ryan Hreljac in Grade 1

That was it! Ryan would ask his parents for the $70 and, Prest-o (his teacher's name was Mrs. Prest), problem solved. His mom and dad would give him the money because they'd love his idea.

Hmmm, not so fast.

Susan and Mark Hreljac liked Ryan's idea, all right, but they weren't about to hand over the cash. No matter how good the idea and no matter how unselfish the reasons, Ryan would have to earn the money. His parents would give him chores around the house and pay him for his work. If he really wanted to build a well in Africa, he would have to prove it by working for it.

Ryan's Grade 1 class at Holy Cross School. Ryan is in the top row, fourth from the left.

His parents had their doubts. After all, Ryan was only six. They figured, sure, for a day or two, maybe even a week or two, Ryan would do the work and save the money. Eventually, though, he would probably lose interest.

But that's not how it went. Ryan worked and worked and then worked some more. He washed windows. Two bucks. He vacuumed. A buck. He picked pinecones at his grandparents' place for change. For a few more dollars, he gathered up branches in his neighborhood after a nasty ice storm. After four months of chores, Ryan had a cookie tin filled with $70 in coins, enough to buy a well in Africa.

Ryan's family, left to right: older brother Jordan, father Mark, Ryan, mother Susan, younger brother Keegan.

Now they had to figure out how to get the money to Africa. After asking various people and government agencies, Ryan and his parents heard about an organization called WaterCan, whose purpose was to help provide safe water in poor countries.

WaterCan seemed perfect, and Ryan's well-earned dream was within reach. When the day came in April 1998 to deliver the money, he dressed in his best clothes, including his favorite Batman and Joker tie. Then Ryan and his mother drove into Ottawa, an hour away, cookie tin in hand.

Since Ryan's appointment with WaterCan was not until the afternoon, he went to his mom's office. Just sitting around would have made the morning last forever, so they put him to work. He sharpened pencils and emptied garbage baskets. At the end of the morning, his mom's boss gave him $5 for his work, which Ryan put straight into his tin. Then they went out for lunch. Ryan had his favorite—pizza and orange pop—but he was so nervous he forgot to wipe off his orange pop mustache.

Finally, they arrived at WaterCan's offices. Just before they opened the door, Ryan squeezed his mom's hand one last time. It would be so good to celebrate the months of hard work.

Then came disappointing news. The people at WaterCan said Ryan's $70, while most welcome, would buy only a hand pump for a well. Building an entire well would cost $2000. Ryan's spirits sank.

Now, $2000 is a lot of money. Besides, the $70 would be put to good use. Ryan should be proud of himself, they said. Not many kids could have done what he had. It was time to go back to regular kid things.

But wait. Ryan just wasn't ready to give up. Recovering from the surprise, he said, "That's okay—I'll just do more chores."

On the way home in the car, Ryan started to plan how he could make enough money to build a whole well. It would just take time. The good news for his parents was they were going to get lots more chores done. But earning $2000 could take Ryan years. Surely he would get bored and give up.

They weren't counting on the ripple effect. A friend of the family was impressed with Ryan's efforts and wrote up his story for the local newspaper. Something about the story of a determined little boy, his $70 and his plan to build a well in Africa caught the attention of all kinds of people, young and old. This was something good, something people could help with. Ripples of good will began to spread.

People started to send money. A check for $25 arrived from a ninety-year-old woman named Margaret in a nearby town. It was the first check Ryan had ever received, and he didn't know what to do with it or that it could be turned into money for his well.

More letters came, and more money. What had once seemed impossible now had a slim chance of success. Awesome things happened. A five year old named Taylor saw a story about Ryan's well on television. He went straight upstairs, smashed his piggy bank and told his mom he wanted to help with the well. Taylor did chores too and ran a lemonade stand. Imagine, a five-year-old boy with a seven-year-old hero (Ryan was now seven).

A man named Walter was also intrigued by Ryan's story, and it just so happened he was involved in drilling for water in Eastern Ontario, where Ryan lived. Walter contacted other people in the drilling business who were part of an association, and they decided to make a big contribution to Ryan's project.

Walter invited Ryan and his family to visit. Ryan and Walter hit it off, even though there were sixty years between them. Walter showed Ryan his huge well-drilling equipment. Ryan was fascinated. Walter found out they were both big fans of the same hockey team. Before they parted, Walter and Ryan had become friends, and Walter handed Ryan a check from his association. The well was becoming a bit more real.

The ripples continued. The well drillers' donation was reported in a story in the newspaper, and it caught the eye of all kinds of organizations and

A man named Walter invited Ryan to see his well-drilling equipment and donated money to help build Ryan's well.

schools. They also wanted to give—and they wanted to meet Ryan. Would he come and talk to them?

Gulp. Umm, okay. Even in school, Ryan was pretty quiet, so talking in front of people would be hard. But if people felt the same way about water as he did, he would just have to do it.

One of the first visits was in the middle of winter to a small village two hours away. Ryan and his mom wondered if they were crazy as they drove through the cold, snowy night. When they got to the meeting hall, Ryan's mom had to turn her briefcase on its side for Ryan to stand on, so he could be seen as he spoke.

Ryan was nervous, but the people were fascinated by the story he told. They donated money to his well. *Hey*, he thought, *I can do this*. And do it he did. He spoke to school classes, church groups and service clubs, and by the end of 1998 Ryan had raised enough money to build his well.

Ryan spoke to groups interested in water. This water drop was a big fan.

WaterCan contacted an organization called Canadian Physicians for Aid and Relief (CPAR) to ask them to find a suitable location for the well. Ryan asked that it be built near a school, so CPAR chose Angolo Primary School near the village of Agweo in Uganda, and in January 1999 Ryan's Well was completed.

But money continued to roll in. Ryan had met Gizaw Shibru, who works for CPAR in Uganda. Gizaw explained that wells in Uganda were drilled by hand, using a tool called an auger. It's like a huge screw that has to be twisted into the ground and pulled out, over and over. It's hard, hot work, and it usually takes more than a dozen people over a week to drill one well. The perfect answer would be a power drill that could be carried around on the back of a truck, Gizaw said, but that would cost about $25 000.

Ryan couldn't get the picture out of his head: a well-drilling rig, cruising from village to village in Africa. He could do that because by now, for Ryan, anything was possible.

In 1999 Ryan's well was built near Agweo, Uganda.

As the news of Ryan's work spread, his classmates in Kemptville were anxious to get involved. His teacher, Lynn Dillabaugh, wanted to help too, and decided to bring her students and the children of Angolo School in Uganda together as pen pals. In January 1999 Ryan and his friends at school wrote to their new pen pals. The letters were packaged up and shipped to Uganda, half a world away. Then they waited. And waited.

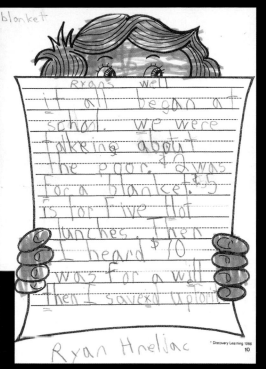

Ryan explains how it all happened.

wed. Jan. 6, 1994
Dear Jimmy, My name is Ryan. I am a 7 year old boy. I have blue eyes. My teacher is Mrs. Dillabaugh. There are three spelling groups The star group and the snoopy group. I am the well builder. What is your name?
your friend,
Ryan.

In 1999 Ryan wrote to his pen pal, Akana Jimmy, for the first time.

Finally, in June, letters from Uganda arrived. Ryan was overjoyed as he unfolded the letter from the pen pal who had been chosen for him.

Ryan and Akana Jimmy began a busy exchange of letters. Over the next year, they asked what each other's home was like ("It must be cool to have a house made out of grass," Ryan wrote in one letter), what food they ate, what sports they liked. Never, ever, did Ryan think he would meet Jimmy. Never, ever, did he think he would see his well.

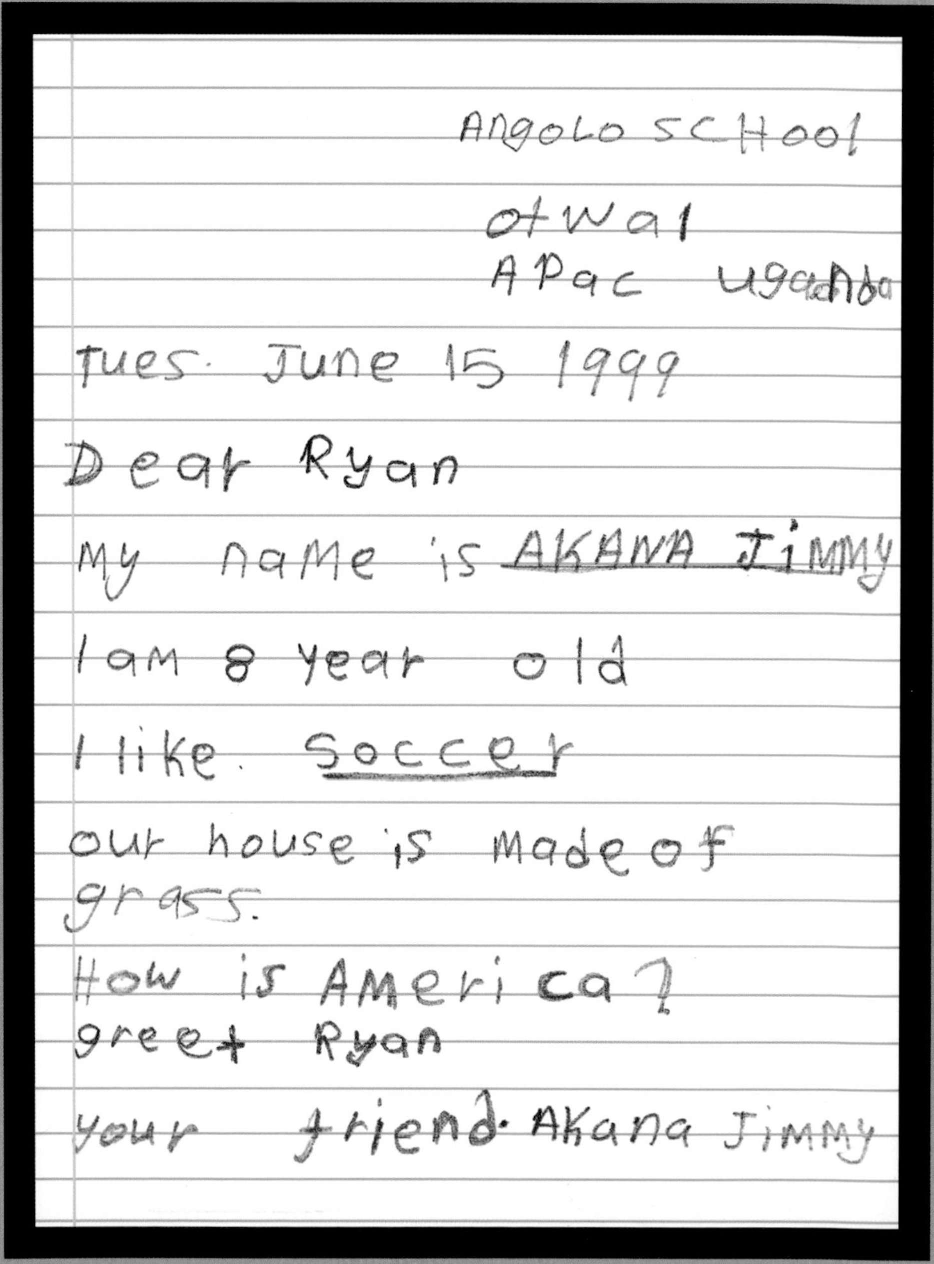

ANGOLO SCHOOL
Otwal
APac Uganda

Tues. June 15 1999

Dear Ryan

My name is AKANA JIMMY

I am 8 year old

I like Soccer

Our house is Made of grass.

How is America?

greet Ryan

your friend. Akana Jimmy

This was the first letter Jimmy wrote to Ryan.

Weird things kept happening, though. People Ryan didn't know kept sending money, people who had read the news stories. Then more stories were written in bigger newspapers. The truck-mounted power drill became more and more possible. There were some interviews on television. People talked to other people. The ripples spread outward. People still wanted to give.

Could they buy a drill and dig more wells? And how far away was Uganda anyway?

Ryan gave more and more speeches about the need for clean water in Africa. He spoke at the Millennium Dreamers Conference at Walt Disney World, Florida, where he was presented with a star on the Disney Walk of Fame.

Three

Agweo village, Uganda, 1999

If there is a place on Earth that you would wish would have clean water, it is Africa. And nowhere more than northern Uganda, the home of Akana Jimmy.

Most of the year, it is a parched land, very dry. Jimmy would come out of his grass and mud hut in the morning to be greeted almost daily by the bright, hot sun, a blessing and a curse. And it is a poor place, where people survive by growing vegetables, such as beans, and raising a few animals, such as goats or chickens. No matter. Northern Uganda was home, the place Jimmy was born and where he would live his life.

It's not exactly certain when Jimmy was born, but the best estimates are that it was in 1989, likely sometime in spring. In his culture, birthdays are not of great importance. There are far more important issues in the daily lives of villagers, such as finding water and growing food.

Jimmy's youth was difficult, even by the standards of his African village. Both of his parents disappeared when he was young and were presumed to be dead. Though the details are not known, it is almost certain their disappearance was connected to a civil war being fought in northern Uganda that started before Jimmy was born.

It is common in many African cultures for relatives to get involved when family members and their children are in need. So it was with Jimmy, who was taken in by his Aunt Sophia after his parents disappeared. Jimmy's four older brothers and three sisters were all either married by this time or had already left the village, in part to avoid the dangers of the civil war.

There were no more than three hundred people in the village, and they all knew one another. Within this tight circle the means of survival were established, shared and passed on.

This is Jimmy about the time he first wrote to his pen pal, Ryan.

When Jimmy moved in, his aunt's home consisted of three huts, with walls made of mud and grass. One hut served as the kitchen and the other two were bedrooms, one for adults and one for children. Each hut, because it is separate, is called a "house," and when Jimmy was ten Aunt Sophia built him a house. Actually, it was just Jimmy's own bedroom, but it was called a house.

Jimmy lived in a house made of mud with a thatched roof, like the ones you see here. Water had to be collected in plastic containers.

Collecting water could take several hours every day.

It takes experience and skill to build a house with mud and grass that can withstand the rains when they come, but these houses were sturdy. There was only one tiny window, about the size of a small book. Too many big windows would let in too much heat.

In the kitchen "house," cooking was done on a fire, and family members would sit cross-legged on the floor to eat. Some houses had rickety furniture, such as a chair or small table. There was no electricity or indoor plumbing. People went to the toilet in the bush.

Going to school was not possible for Jimmy at first. There was no money for school fees, and even if there had been, living with his aunt meant he had to help pay his way by doing chores. Tending her garden was one task, as was gathering water, which is a major responsibility, especially for a child aged five, six or seven.

There is some water around Jimmy's village during the rainy season, but there are long periods in the year when water is scarce. Then children, including Jimmy, would have to walk up to 5 km (3 mi.) each way to get water. Jimmy sometimes made that walk four or five times a day. And it was not as if you could always go to a specific spot for the water. You had to look for it. When you found it you had to carry it back.

There was also the problem with the water itself. Sometimes the water was brown and smelled bad. "You drank it just because you were thirsty," Jimmy says. "You closed your eyes and held your nose. You did it because there was nothing else." Besides the color and the awful smell, the water often made your insides hurt.

Even though he had not attended school, Jimmy was a smart boy, and he proved it when he finally got the opportunity to go to school in 1997. Jimmy was starting school at an age — about eight— when kids in other parts of the world had already been in school for as long as four years.

This boy is lucky enough to have a family bicycle that he can use to transport water.

The drinking water is murky and bad smelling and sometimes contains bacteria that make people sick.

Women gather water from a small pond.

At Angolo Primary School, where Jimmy went, most of his class of about one hundred pupils sat on the floor. Some classes had four desks that each held four or five kids. Sometimes classes were held outside under a tree so the children could be in the shade.

Before Ryan's well was built, there were seven hundred kids at the school. A year and a half later, there were two thousand students from all over ... all because of the well. The well meant Jimmy and the other children didn't have to spend hours every day searching for water and hauling it home. More teachers were hired. Eventually there were twelve teachers for the two thousand children.

The school had books, but they had to be shared, which became more difficult as the number of students grew. Everyone had to cooperate.

Jimmy studied science, social studies, math and English. (At home he spoke the local language, Lwo.) Jimmy did well in school, considering he had such a late start. With the exception of math, he passed all subjects consistently. It helped that he liked all his subjects, even math.

On the way to Angolo Primary School, near the village of Agweo

This is Angolo Primary School, which grew to hold 2000 students.

In school, geography, history and social studies focused on Africa and Uganda. For instance, Jimmy and his classmates learned about Idi Amin, a former president of Uganda who was an evil ruler and caused much damage throughout the country. The pupils also studied about apartheid, the former racist policy in South Africa that kept white and black people separate. But they never studied about the rebels who were waging civil war in northern Uganda. They only talked about the rebels outside class, among themselves.

Jimmy loved school, but it was unlikely that he could go far with his education. In fact, few people in Jimmy's village go beyond Grade 7, mostly because high school and university studies are expensive.

After school, once the chores were done and the water was fetched, the children played sports. Football, as soccer is called in Uganda, was the big thing. Jimmy often played football, and he was also a very fast runner.

By the time Ryan's well was drilled, Jimmy was enjoying school and doing well. He was chosen as Ryan's pen pal because he was one of the brightest pupils in his class and because of his friendly personality. He couldn't believe his good fortune. With each letter from Ryan, he learned more about this faraway place called Canada.

Perhaps best of all was the new well, Ryan's well. When it was finished in 1999, it brought beautiful, clean water up out of the ground. The well was a gift from his pen pal, a boy just like him.

Jimmy longed for a chance to thank Ryan in person for this gift of life—clean water.

This well is similar to the one near Angolo School. It's not much to look at, but easy access to clean water changes peoples' lives.

Agweo village, Uganda, Summer 2000

Four

For Ryan Hreljac, this would be a day to remember forever.

That morning Ryan opened his sleepy eyes a tiny bit and, squinting cautiously, looked about. Bare brick walls stared back. Where was the picture of his beloved Ottawa Senators hockey team? *Uganda!* he thought, leaping out of bed. *This is the real deal!*

A dream that had seemed so unlikely was about to come true. He was going to see his well. He was going to drink from his well. And he was going to meet his pen pal, Akana Jimmy.

Getting from Canada to Uganda had taken a lot of work and a lot of help from others. Neighbors had generously donated their airline points for plane tickets. CPAR, the organization that had helped get the well dug, had planned the visit.

On their way to Uganda, Ryan and his parents stopped over in London, England. Ryan's mother got a serious infection that night, but they got treatment for her. Ryan himself went sleepwalking three times, he was so excited. The third time he was almost out in the hall of their hotel before his parents caught him. What if he went sleepwalking in Africa?

Finally, two days after leaving home, including twenty hours of flying, they arrived at the CPAR camp. They had traveled about 16 000 km (10 000 mi.), and now they were just 25 km (15 mi.) from Agweo, where the well was located. The drive to the village would still take more than an hour— the roads were mostly just two rough tracks, with tall grass on both sides.

The jeeps crept along, rocking and rolling in the rutted tracks. The slow pace made the anticipation soar even more. Ryan had butterflies in his stomach.

As the jeeps drew closer to the village, more and more people wandered up to the road to watch them pass. "Reeaann, Reeaann," they chanted. Later, someone from CPAR said that people for miles around knew Ryan's name.

Finally — it had seemed forever to Ryan — the jeep turned the corner and the lines of people came into view.

Ryan and his father began their long walk, with the camera crew filming every step.

A Canadian television crew became interested in Ryan's efforts to raise money for a well and decided to follow him to Uganda.

The clapping dipped and soared, but it never stopped. It was loud at first, then, as they went past smaller children, it got quieter. Back among bigger kids it would get loud again. Finally the long walk was over, and Ryan met Jimmy. Then Ryan saw the well.

To look at, any well is no big deal. It's the same with Ryan's well. There's a pump and a platform, and the splashed water and red soil combined to make an interesting color of mud. But to the villagers, the well was priceless and a thing of beauty.

This is Ryan's well.

The people of the village had carefully planned what was going to happen. First, Ryan was to cut a ribbon to declare the well open. That proved to be harder than it sounded. Ryan fumbled a bit, but with Jimmy's help managed to snip the ribbon. Then Ryan pumped some water into a bottle to bring back to Canada.

After the ribbon cutting, it was time to celebrate. Dancing, singing and feasts had been planned by the school's headmaster. As guests of honor, Ryan and his parents sat on chairs front and center. A homemade plastic canopy had been set up to keep them out of the sun. Still, the heat was nearly unbearable for what turned out to be four hours of entertainment.

As pen pal and the villager chosen to host and accompany Ryan, Jimmy beamed as he too sat with the special visitors in the shade. Simba, the lion woman, a village elder, got things started as she danced and chanted her welcome. The entertainment, Jimmy explained, was the villagers' way of telling stories. Those stories were about CPAR and Canada, about themselves and their villages, their culture and traditions and also about their special guest who had brought them water. It was a privilege for villagers to be chosen to tell their stories to Ryan, so they performed like never before. It was quite a show.

The importance of the occasion was clear from the colorful costumes of the performers and the energy and excitement of the dances. One group of women singers wore purple and orange skirts. Another group sported headbands, belts and anklets made of grasses as they danced around drummers. All the villagers laughed like crazy when Ryan tried to figure out the dance and join in. He was a good sport.

The singing was unlike anything Ryan had ever heard. Sometimes, it sounded like chanting and

Dancers entertain Ryan and his family at the celebration to open Ryan's well.

talking. Other times it was mostly lots of people humming softly together.

There were speeches by village leaders, such as the headmaster. And Jimmy welcomed Ryan in a speech in English that he had practiced over and over.

Ryan spoke too. He told the villagers how he earned the money to build his well. He told them he had also brought enough money for the headmaster, Mr. George Opiny, to buy seventy-one desks for the school. He said his school had held a hike-a-thon and raised enough money to buy kits containing school supplies for every student at Angolo School. He also explained that his father was a police officer whose colleagues had given him some money for the trip, so he had brought soccer balls.

This plaque, decorated with seeds and beans, was presented to Ryan.

27

He finished by saying: "I can't believe I have my well in Uganda now, right here at Angolo Primary School ... If we all work together I think we can make the whole world a great place for everyone!"

During a pause in the celebrations, Ryan was interviewed by the TV crew who had accompanied them. At one point, there was a long, drawn-out *aaaaaaggggggghhhhhhhh* sound in the background. Ryan heard it, was puzzled by it, but carried on. The director said it sounded like something was dying behind them. Sure enough, when they finished the interview, the director looked at the tape and said they would have to do the interview again. A goat had just been slaughtered in the background—that was the sound they'd heard, and it was all on tape.

The goat was part of the menu for the feast that followed. The villagers had gone all out. There were different meats, such as chicken and, of course, goat. (The goat was very tender.) There were lots and lots of vegetables, many of them new to the Canadians. Jimmy said the kinds of food and the amount provided proved how much this day meant to his village.

Being the guest and a little brave, Ryan dove into some of the African food. Not all of it was scrumptious. Some things were just too strange for his Canadian tastes. A few things he just couldn't eat at all, and one, which was white and a kind of "banana mush," made him feel like he might throw up. But at least he had tried.

Finally, at the end of the long day, an exhausted but happy Ryan and his family and escorts got ready to head back to the CPAR camp where they were staying. Ryan said goodbye to Jimmy, but not for long. Jimmy and Ryan had got along so well that some people decided to try to get them together again.

The next day Ryan hopped on the back of a

The people of Agweo gave Ryan a goat as a present. He named it Peace. But Peace couldn't come to Canada. Peace remained at the nearby CPAR camp.

motorcycle to be driven back to the village, where he spent the day with Jimmy and his friends in school.

There's an interesting picture of this day in school in which Ryan's blond head pops up in the middle of a sea of studious black faces. Ryan played soccer and other games with the children. He actually participated in classes too. He says it was one of the most memorable school days he has ever had.

It looked like Jimmy and Ryan would have to part, this time for good. But some sneaky adults had another plan. They had made arrangements with Jimmy's aunt to let Jimmy come back to the CPAR camp with Ryan.

Ryan attends school with Jimmy at Angolo School.

At the camp, the boys played more soccer and other games with the local children. The CPAR workers said they'd never had kids at the camp, but after Ryan arrived, children started hanging around, looking for games of soccer and volleyball. Later, as it got dark, Ryan taught Jimmy some card games, including one called War, which they played over and over. The boys joked and jostled like long-lost friends. It seemed like they had known each other forever.

When bedtime finally rolled around, Ryan's parents asked Jimmy if he wanted his own room or if he wanted to share with Ryan.

"Ryan," he said without a pause.

Ryan's parents had brought Jimmy a present, a book about Uganda. Jimmy stayed up late into the night reading it by flashlight.

The next morning seemed to come all too soon. It was time for Jimmy to go back to Agweo and for Ryan and his family to say their goodbyes to the villagers before heading home to Canada.

The pupils had prepared a farewell chant to wish their guests a safe journey home.

"We have come to the time that we have to part with our very best friend, Ryan," said the headmaster. "The people of Angolo are so grateful, they are taking Ryan as their son and brother."

Ryan and Jimmy had become friends, which made leaving all the more difficult.

He said that that day, July 27, would be called Ryan's Day every year from then on.

All that didn't change the fact it was a very sad parting.

"Everyone was smiling," Ryan's mom recalls, "but no one was happy."

Ryan didn't cry, but his face was glum. He wanted to stay and spend more time with Jimmy.

"I remember when we were leaving I had this awful feeling in my stomach that we were never going to see this kid again," Ryan's dad said of Jimmy. "We'd taken all these lovely pictures and done all this stuff, and I just couldn't help thinking: this kid's got nothing. I felt so awful."

Mark Hreljac was right to feel awful. After such a happy time, life was going to take a serious turn for the worse for Jimmy.

After leaving Ryan's well, the Hreljacs traveled to Massaba mountain. There, Ryan was given the African name, "Massaba."

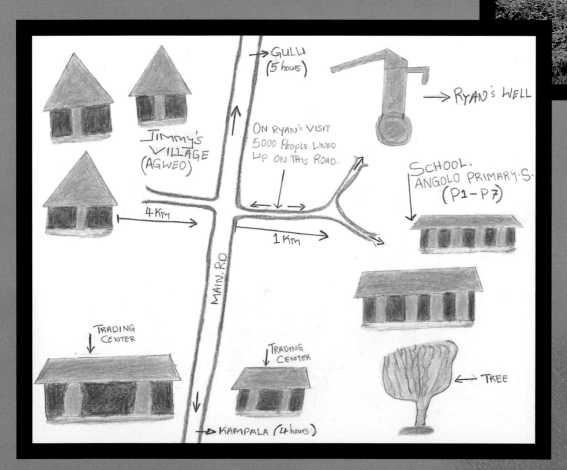

This is Jimmy's drawing of his village and Ryan's well.

Five

"When I was running, they tried to chase me. They didn't catch me. They tried to shoot me with the guns but I was far away."

Agweo village, Uganda, Fall 2002

Screams pierced the night air, startling Jimmy out of a deep sleep. Shouting and yelling exploded at the doorway to his hut. Outside, women and children were crying. And then the frightening smell of gunpowder filled Jimmy's nostrils and told him the worst was happening.

The rebels were back in all their fury. That was especially bad news for Jimmy because he was exactly the kind of person they were looking for.

The Lord's Resistance Army (LRA) had been fighting a rebel war against the government of Uganda for almost twenty years, forcing young children like Jimmy to become soldiers.

The LRA hunted for children at night, under cover of darkness. When villagers suspected an attack, they would send the children to nearby towns, where they came to be known as Night Commuters, or into the woods. They would return to the village in the morning, when the danger had passed. In spite of these precautions, many children were captured.

If you were captured and managed to escape, the LRA would come after you again. But the second time, they wouldn't take you captive—they would kill you. Jimmy had already managed to avoid the rebels once during an earlier raid by hiding, and the rebels knew it. This time if he was captured …

These chilling thoughts raced through Jimmy's mind as he huddled in his hut with his cousins Daniel, James, Isaac and Milly. He knew it was hopeless. The air was thick with fear. The rebels, though young, would show them no mercy. They needed new soldier "recruits"— Jimmy's greatest fear.

The LRA was led by a strange and, many say, crazy man named Joseph Kony. His philosophy is based on tribal mysticism and ten commandments, but not the Ten Commandments of the Bible.

Kony's version includes beliefs such as witchcraft.

Child soldiers are used by Kony to enforce his "thinking." They are beaten and worse if they don't obey. It is estimated that more than twenty thousand children have been abducted by the LRA, whose soldiers are so brutal they often force these children to kill their own parents.

Jimmy had witnessed family and friends being abducted. He knew the rebels had something to do with the disappearance of his parents. He knew he wanted nothing to do with the barbaric LRA.

Flashlight beams probed the inside of the hut. "Get up! Get up!" the soldiers shouted. Jimmy's heart pounded. There was nowhere to run. Resistance was pointless — Jimmy and his family members were unarmed and outnumbered.

The soldiers tied Jimmy's hands together, then looped the rope behind his back and tied it to his cousin Isaac. The boys were marched out of the hut.

Jimmy feared for his life — and for that of his cousin, who was older than the LRA preferred for soldiers. That could mean they would kill Isaac.

As the captives were marched to the middle of the village, Jimmy noticed a tiny bit of slack in the rope tying his hands. He wiggled his wrist and found he could twist it slightly. He wiggled it some more and got a bit more slack. He was able to sneak the knot up to his mouth. He chewed and pulled to loosen it. With a bit of luck, the rope would become slack enough for him to work on the knot with his hands.

Wait a minute, wait a minute! Jimmy dropped his hands back down in front of him. *Is this a trap? Are they setting me up so that when I escape they can shoot me?* What did it matter? It was his only chance.

He looked over at Isaac, who seemed to understand his plan. To make sure, Jimmy looked down at the knot and wriggled his hand as if giving a demonstration. Isaac looked away. *He looked away!* Jimmy couldn't believe it. Had Isaac given up?

Jimmy had no time to come up with a new plan. In minutes, the rebels would lead the captives out of the village and begin the long trek deep into the wilds of northern Uganda.

Jimmy started on the ropes again. With every movement of his hand, he seemed to get freer.

Then, for no clear reason, Isaac gave a sudden start, as if something had scared him. The movement caught a soldier's attention just as Jimmy was working on the rope. Had he been seen? If they discovered how close he was to breaking free, they'd shoot him on the spot.

The soldier, barely older than Jimmy, approached them. He glared at Isaac with suspicion and gave him a shove, just to show him who was boss. Jimmy held his breath, expecting the worst. But the guard turned away and wandered back to join the other soldiers. Jimmy let out his breath. His attempts to free his hands had not been detected. A moment later, the order came for the prisoners to prepare to head out.

Jimmy had to act. If he was going to make a break for it, it had to be here, in territory he knew like the back of his hand. That was his one advantage.

As the line of prisoners started to move, Jimmy finally freed his hands. It was now or never. Again he glanced over at Isaac, but his cousin made it clear he wasn't coming along. Jimmy was stunned. He would have to go it alone.

Jimmy was in the middle of the group, far enough away from the soldiers at the front and back to make his break. He estimated there was a distance of about half a soccer field when he would be in the open before he reached the tall grass and bush. With luck and the element of surprise, he could be halfway there before anyone noticed. It would take all of his running and dodging skills to save his life. This was it. Jimmy closed his eyes and gathered his courage, then, feeling like he was going to throw up, he took off.

One step, two steps, top speed. Halfway to the bush and still no response from the soldiers. It was just as he had hoped. Sweat poured off his forehead.

Then came a shout, and within seconds a bullet whizzed by his head. Then another bullet, this time past his shoulder. He zigged and zagged and ducked. The soldiers were having trouble aiming at him. It was working.

Jimmy heard soldiers running, but he had made it to the edge of the dense grass. He plunged in. Now it was advantage Jimmy— he knew every bump, bush and hole. He ran until he was certain the rebels could not track him. Finally, he collapsed to the ground, his thoughts still racing.

"I knew if I didn't run, they would kill me. I had one choice, run or be killed. That's why I ran. I knew they were bad. And even if they didn't kill me, they would have made me fight and kill my people."

In the distance, Jimmy could still hear gunshots, but they were not getting closer. In time, the night grew still, interrupted only by the occasional gunshot. His breathing was slowing to a regular pace, as was his heartbeat. His forehead was cooling down. Scary thoughts stopped ping-ponging around his head.

Lying beneath the huge, majestic African night sky usually made him feel so free. But not now. He felt trapped because his future was a huge question mark. *What's next?*

In the distance an orange glow appeared on the horizon. It grew brighter and brighter, and Jimmy realized what was happening. As they so often do, the rebels were burning the village to the ground, destroying the homes of his friends and family. They already had so little. Now they would have nothing.

Jimmy had never felt so helpless.

"I ran and fell down, ran and fell down, ran and fell down to avoid the bullets."

35

Six

Kemptville, Ontario, Fall 2002

The Hreljacs were worried. Reports from Uganda were telling a frightening story. The rebels were raiding more often and deeper into northern Uganda, and they were all around Jimmy's village.

Though he didn't understand everything, eleven-year-old Ryan knew his pen pal Jimmy was in danger. Late in June a letter arrived from Jimmy, confirming the rebel threat: "We are not learning very well this term. The rebels make us afraid. Sometimes we miss school because of this."

Ryan was worried about his pen pal Jimmy, especially when a letter arrived from Jimmy saying that the rebel army was nearby.

HOLY CROSS SCHOOL
KEMPTVILLE
ONTARIO
CANADA.
29th June. 2002

Dear Ryan,

I received your letters on Friday 17th May 2002. I was Very, Very happy to receive from you and our new friend mariela.

I am fine and So are my family and others. We are not learning Very well this Term. The rebels make Us afraid. Sometimes We miss School because of this.

Last term I was Second in my class. I am

It was hard to understand, in peaceful Kemptville, that a rebel army was disrupting school on the other side of the world. Because normally life in Kemptville was pretty quiet. But not lately. Not for Ryan Hreljac anyway. Now it wasn't just local schools and organizations that wanted Ryan to speak about his well. People were inviting him all over the world.

He was traveling with his parents to places such as South Africa, Australia and Japan for conferences where he was the center of attention, the keynote speaker. He appeared on *The Oprah Winfrey Show*. The best part was that the money he was raising was going to build wells in many parts of Africa. To make sure the money went where it was supposed to, Ryan and his parents had set up the Ryan's Well Foundation.

All through the summer and into the fall, the Hreljacs stayed in touch with people they had met in Uganda. They were eager for news about Jimmy. Then came a chilling e-mail from a close friend, Tom Omach, a Ugandan who worked for CPAR. "September-October was a very bad time … The LRA rebels attacked the sub-country and killed over 30 people. All the schools including Angolo Primary have been closed."

The news got worse. "On October 25," Tom continued, "I visited Otwal [the area around Agweo] … We were told that Jimmy was abducted but he managed to escape. However, two of his cousins were killed and another two were abducted."

And then a sigh of relief: Tom had found Jimmy. He had lost everything, but he was alive. And Tom was trying to get Jimmy into boarding school in the town of Lira.

Tom succeeded, and the Hreljacs, relieved to know Jimmy was safe, decided to pay his school fees. His best chance, they felt, was to get an education.

By 2002 Ryan was speaking at conferences all over the world, including the World Summit on Sustainable Development in South Africa.

Ryan's Well Foundation was set up to raise money for wells in Africa.

Boarding school was good for Jimmy. There was no water to fetch or chores to do. He could concentrate on his studies, and he did well. He lived at the school during the week and stayed with his Uncle Amos or Tom Omach on weekends. But bit by bit the situation got worse as the rebels pushed nearer.

Soon even Lira was no longer safe. Sometimes Jimmy and the other students had to leave the boarding school and sleep in the bush far away. The rebels didn't come every day, but when they did, they would stay for days and the children had to stay in the bush until they finally left. Jimmy knew his situation was particularly bad: he had escaped the rebels twice, and they would make him pay.

Back in Canada, the Hreljacs were so worried that they started thinking seriously about bringing Jimmy to Canada. But how? Jimmy didn't have a birth certificate, let alone a passport. And even if they could get him a passport, they weren't sure he would be allowed into the country.

Then a bit of luck. Ryan was scheduled to speak at an international health conference in Vancouver in May 2003 on the importance of clean water in developing countries. Maybe Jimmy could participate as a guest from Uganda. Finally there was hope. It was time to break the news to Jimmy.

Jimmy was shocked and excited. In the back of his mind, he had sometimes let himself think about visiting Ryan, but it always seemed impossible. Now he was going. All the way ... to Canada!

Jimmy didn't have a clue what he needed to do to get to Canada, but fortunately Tom Omach was there to guide him. The first step was to get Jimmy a passport and visa, which meant a trip to the capital city of Uganda, Kampala.

It was a slow, four-hour drive to Kampala, a city of 2.5 million people. What a difference from Jimmy's village of three hundred! As they wound their way

through the outskirts, Jimmy was amazed and overwhelmed by the hustle and bustle of the city.

Tom set about making travel arrangements. At times he would leave Jimmy outside an office or business while he went inside. "Don't move," he would tell Jimmy, but he was wasting his words. Jimmy never budged. He was too scared to move. It was like he was cemented to the spot.

In Kampala, everything was strange, even the language. Although this was the capital city of his own country, people spoke a different version of his language, which he didn't understand. Surrounded by thousands of people, Jimmy still felt very much alone.

Tom realized he needed to do more than paperwork to get Jimmy ready to travel. He had to teach Jimmy how to look after himself, how to survive. No time like the present. He sent Jimmy into a store to buy some clothes for the trip. Jimmy managed, though the clothes didn't fit or match. But it was a start.

The biggest hurdle was getting the visa that would allow Jimmy to enter Canada. Tom knew there would be long lineups, so the two of them arrived at the visa office at four o'clock in the morning. They waited as the sun came up, and all through the heat of the day, but still they didn't get into the office before it closed. The next morning they went an hour earlier. Success!

Just when all the arrangements were made and Jimmy was ready to leave, disaster struck. Jimmy would have to stop over in London, England, on his way to Canada. To do so, he would need something called a transit visa. Jimmy's stopover would last sixteen hours, but a transit visa could only be issued for twelve hours. His application was denied. It looked as if all Tom's work had been for nothing.

The Hreljacs got on the case. They talked to people in the Canadian prime minister's office,

Tom Omach, on the left, had been involved with water projects for many years. His newest project: getting Jimmy to Canada.

who tried to help. They talked to people in the British High Commission in Ottawa. Everyone was sympathetic, but nothing worked.

The departure time for Jimmy's flight to Canada drew closer and closer ... and passed. Jimmy's dream vanished. There would be no visit to Canada, no seeing Ryan again. Despondent, he made his way back to Lira.

But Ryan's parents were not ready to give up, nor was Tom Omach. Tom had to get a new visa for the trip. And now, time was the enemy: the date of the conference, the reason for Jimmy's visit to Canada, was drawing closer.

Finally things started to fall into place. Because officials were familiar with the earlier visa problems, Jimmy got his transit visa. A new plane ticket was purchased. Everything was ready.

There was just one minor detail: Jimmy was missing. He was not in his village, and they were having trouble finding him at his boarding school. Where was he? And could he be found in time for his flight?

In Canada, it was nail-biting time again as the second departure date drew nearer. Then, the day before Jimmy was supposed to fly to Canada, they got word from Tom. Jimmy had been found. He would be on the plane.

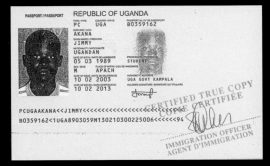

This is Jimmy's passport. His actual birth date is not known, so officials had to guess at the date.

This is the famous visa that finally allowed Jimmy to get on a plane heading for London, England, and then Canada.

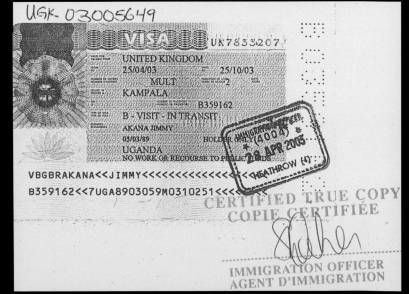

40

Toronto, Ontario, April 29, 2003

Kampala, Uganda, to London, England, to Toronto, Canada—after almost two days of travel, the plane delivering Akana Jimmy to Canada rolled up to the gate at the airport in Toronto.

Now what? thought Jimmy. He was tired and confused. And hungry. On the plane, friendly people had offered him lots of food, but none of it was familiar. For one thing, they kept trying to feed him something that looked and tasted like grass (it was actually salad).

On the flight from Kampala to London, Jimmy had been lucky to sit with another Ugandan boy, Oyo Patrick. Patrick was about Jimmy's age, and he was also traveling alone. The two boys talked the whole way. It helped to pass time and calm nerves.

After staying overnight in London with friends of Ryan's family, Jimmy had boarded the seven-hour flight to Toronto. This time, without Patrick beside him, he was a little scared.

Now the plane had stopped and the doors slid open. People were grabbing their packs and parcels and leaving the plane. Jimmy just sat there—he didn't know what to do. The flight crew tried to help him. Who was meeting him? He fumbled to answer in his limited English: "Ryan." But no one knew who Ryan was. (In his confusion, Jimmy forgot he had instructions in his pocket.)

Seven

```
                        DUPLICATE                     0001 OF 0001
BRITISH AIRWAYS E-TICKET RECEIPT / ITINERARY  DATE: 25APR03
ENDORSEMENTS: NONREF/YOUTHVALID BA ONLY DOB 05.03.  ISSUED BY:894 90170
9                                             BRITISH AIRWAYS KLA
                                              KAMPALA
NAME:  AKANA/JIMMYMR(ADT)                      BOOKING REF  X9EF55
FROM              TO                    FLIGHT  CL DATE  TIME ST BA
ENTEBBE           EBB LONDON LHR        LHR BA 0062  V 28APR 0920 OK 2P
LONDON LHR        LHR TORONTO INTL      YYZ BA 0093  V 29APR 1130 OK 2P
TORONTO INTL      YYZ LONDON LHR        LHR BA 0096  V 06SEP 2335 OK 2
LONDON LHR        LHR ENTEBBE          EBB BA 0063  V 07SEP 1935 OK 2-

FARE:USD 1350.00
TAXES/FEES/CHARGES      FORM OF PAYMENT           CONDITIONS OF
   UL    40.00         CASH                       CARRIAGE MAY BE
   YQ     8.00                                    INSPECTED ON
   XT    61.00                                    APPLICATION TO
   TOTAL  USD    1459.00  E-TICKET NBR:125 2408116596   BRITISH AIRWAY
```

Jimmy's plane ticket. It looks so ordinary and yet it took so much to get it.

Jimmy remembered Mark Hreljac, Ryan's dad, as a big guy. That made him easy to spot at Toronto airport.

Riley "protects" the Hreljacs' home. To Jimmy the house looked like a castle.

Eventually a woman from the airline led him by the hand to the arrivals area. Jimmy scanned the faces for someone familiar. Ryan might be hard to spot in the crowd, but he remembered that Mark Hreljac, Ryan's dad, was tall. He would stand out.

He spotted Mark right away.

"Jimmy!" Mark hollered. Jimmy found himself engulfed in a bear hug.

Jimmy looked around. "Where's Ryan?"

Mark explained that Ryan was waiting at home, a four-hour drive away. Jimmy's heart sank. He had been hoping his friend would meet him at the airport. Now Jimmy knew how Ryan must have felt when he wasn't there to meet him in Agweo.

On the drive to Ryan's home, Jimmy's excitement battled his huge need for sleep. He had hardly slept for two days. But how could he sleep now? His dream was coming true. Eventually, though, the darkening sky of the early evening, the smooth humming of the car and his exhaustion won, and Jimmy fell into a happy, deep sleep.

Mark relaxed, too. For the first time in months, Jimmy was safe.

Ryan's family lives in the country in a big two-story house with four bedrooms. But to Jimmy, as they drove up the driveway, it was beyond big. It was massive, a castle.

The whole Hreljac family was waiting for Jimmy. He had never met Jordan and Keegan, Ryan's brothers. If you think it was a calm, quiet meeting, then your house doesn't have a Keegan in it. Keegan, the youngest, started yipping and yelling as soon as the car hit the driveway. By the time Jimmy reached the door, it was chaos.

Keegan took a run across the kitchen and leapt into Jimmy's arms. Through the racket, Jimmy's eyes zeroed in on Ryan. At last! The two friends hugged, then everyone hugged Jimmy. Amazingly, nobody fell over the dog, Riley, who was right in the middle of things. Riley didn't waste any time becoming pals with the newcomer, either.

Ryan and his brothers Jordan (center top) and Keegan (center bottom) welcomed Jimmy with open arms.

The Hreljac family with
Akana Jimmy

For someone used to living in a mud hut with only the barest essentials, the Hreljac home was something from another world. It had machines for keeping food cold, for cooking food and even for washing up afterward. There was a big television, a stereo and a computer. There were three bathrooms and another bathtub outside that Ryan told him was called a hot tub.

Then Ryan took Jimmy to a door in the kitchen that opened to stairs going down. This was weird. What was the point of digging such a big hole in the ground, just to put a house on top of it? It was the basement, Ryan explained. "Over there," he pointed, "that's where we play video games. That room across the way, that's Jordan's. I sleep upstairs and so does Keegan. And over there is your room."

My room? Jimmy peered in. It had a desk, some books and a bed and, yes, it was all Jimmy's. *Wow!* But Jimmy was still a little afraid, so he slept with Ryan for a week before moving into his own room. That first night, as Jimmy drifted off to sleep, it felt so good to think he would wake up in the morning and Ryan would be there.

Pen pals reunited

Eight

There was so much to learn. It helped that Jimmy had plunged into a family of boys who could show him the ropes—and share their clothes. It was spring and still cool, and Jimmy's African clothes were just not warm enough. Fortunately he was about the same size as Ryan. One of his favorites was a Toronto Raptors jacket Jimmy got from Susan's brother, who also happens to be named Jimmy.

Jimmy grew to like the cool weather, and he loved being outdoors. He took to walking Riley, who had become his close buddy. Getting away from people on dog walks was a relief—Jimmy was still not confident with his English, and talking was a strain. Sometimes people would laugh at things he said or that he just didn't understand. It was all so new.

After only a couple of weeks in Canada, Jimmy was back on a plane, this time to the conference in Vancouver with Ryan and his mom. And there were more new things. Staying in a hotel was cool, especially the hotel pool. Imagine! A huge pool filled with water—just for playing.

Jimmy attended the conference along with Ryan. While he couldn't follow all the speeches, it was obvious that Ryan was important. Hundreds and hundreds of adults—doctors and officials—listened so closely to a kid ... who happened to be his best friend. Jimmy was proud for Ryan.

Ryan's speech was about the importance of water. In particular, he talked about people in poor countries and described how anybody can help. Some day, Jimmy thought, when he felt more confident about his English, he would tell the same story right beside Ryan. For now, though, all he could do was smile and nod.

Jimmy stuck to Ryan like glue at the conference.

At the Vancouver conference, Jimmy and Ryan test out the hotel pool.

Jimmy smiles for the camera (a bit nervously) on his first day of school.

Back in Kemptville, it was time for school. Jimmy was to spend the last two months of the school year in Grade 8. The first day of school is always a big day, but it was a real challenge for someone used to Angolo Primary School in Uganda.

Jimmy got lost, looking for his classroom. Speaking and listening to English all day was exhausting, and the subjects were all new. But Jimmy was determined. When Jimmy's teachers saw just how determined he was, they gave him extra help—and extra work. The extra work didn't bother Jimmy, and it meant his speaking and schoolwork improved quickly.

One area where Jimmy was successful right away was in track and field. It was obvious to everyone that he was a strong runner. One problem, though, was that he had only ever run in bare feet, but now the rules said he had to wear shoes. Jimmy couldn't get used to shoes, so he did what he calls a "trick." He would start a race in shoes, then stop to kick them off. Even so, he was always one of the top finishers.

Jimmy the runner

There was something odd about his running style. He ran with his left hand down at his side. When his coach asked why, Jimmy explained that it was the way he had learned to run in Africa, while carrying containers of water. They changed that "technique," and it made him even faster.

Jimmy was fast, but he was never first to finish. People began to notice that he would not run ahead of others on his team. When Mark asked him about it, Jimmy said he didn't want to embarrass them. Mark explained it was okay to run ahead, as long as you respect the other racers.

Running made Jimmy proud of himself in his new world. It was something he did well, and, along with support from family and friends and coaches, it helped him feel that he belonged.

At home, things had settled into a routine. Jimmy was now one of four boys competing for washroom time in the morning, for food on the table and for the television remote, though to be fair, Jimmy preferred to let the others go first at things.

Horsing around in the kitchen

47

First marshmallow roast

Soon summer holidays arrived with more new experiences. The family, including Jimmy, visited relatives. It seemed Ryan was always introducing cousins, grandmothers, aunts and uncles to Jimmy, who wondered how he was going to keep all the names straight. He had his first marshmallow roast while visiting relatives in Nova Scotia, caught his first glimpse of Niagara Falls and even tried tubing to beat the heat. That summer, he certainly got a taste of Canada.

First visit to Niagara Falls

Ryan tries tubing, too!

Tubing

First snowman-building, with help from Keegan

First attempt at kite flying

In the fall, as Jimmy prepared to enter Grade 9, time was running out on his visitor's visa. Ryan's parents had been keeping an eye on events in Uganda, and it was clear that the danger was still very real. Over the months, as Jimmy's language improved, he had told them more and more about the situation. They worried now that by returning him to Uganda they would be sending him to his death.

One letter from Tom Omach made them especially anxious. It said: "Jimmy's life is in great danger as the rebels have vowed to hunt for him until he is abducted or killed … if you can keep Jimmy in Canada you will give him a chance …"

There was no choice but to act. Mark and Susan wondered how their boys would feel about making Jimmy's visit permanent. He'd be like their brother. No, he'd *be* their brother. Without hesitation, the boys said: "do what it takes to keep him here."

There was no question: Ryan, Keegan and Jordan wanted Jimmy to stay.

They decided Jimmy would try to claim refugee status. That's a process where people from other countries apply to stay in Canada because they would be in danger if they returned to their home country. Jimmy, the Hreljacs and their lawyer would have to prove that his life was in danger. This was a lot of work. Letters and other documents were gathered from Africa and around Canada. People provided statements about the threats to Jimmy's life. A former Canadian government minister wrote a letter of support.

The lawyer recommended they try for something called an "expedited hearing," which is a faster-than-normal process. Instead of going before an entire immigration tribunal of several people, cases are decided by a single judge. It was riskier — one person, the judge, would decide Jimmy's fate — but the lawyer thought Jimmy would have a good chance because he was a minor (under sixteen).

Then one day the lawyer called to tell them an opening had come up to hear Jimmy's case. Only there wouldn't be a translator, so Jimmy would have to address the judge in English.

The day of the refugee hearing everybody's nerves were jangled. Weeks of planning and months of worry — and a boy's life — were on the line.

Jimmy was very nervous. He didn't understand all that was going on, but he knew it would mean he could stay — or not. Somehow, he had to try hard to tell his story in his best English.

The judge would ask direct questions. Jimmy hoped he could remember what Mark and Susan and the lawyer had told him: Take your time, use words you are comfortable with, we'll try to help when we can.

The judge first questioned Susan. Had the Hreljacs intended to apply for refugee status even before Jimmy arrived? She explained that they

were not sure, but that they had been concerned about Jimmy's safety in Uganda for some time.

The judge then asked Jimmy what had happened the night the rebels attacked. Jimmy thought back to that horrible night. He closed his eyes, trying to remember everything. He spoke slowly about his capture and escape. As he told his story, he was thinking about Ryan, his "brothers," Mark and Susan and his new friends. He didn't want to let them down.

Then it was over. The hearing hadn't taken long, maybe an hour. Was that a good sign? How long does it usually take?

The room was bursting with emotion, a mixture of relief that the hearing was over and concern for the outcome. What would the decision be? Now they were on the edges of their seats.

The judge rose slowly, and, as he came around the corner of the table, he began to smile. He put out his hand and said, "Welcome to Canada, Jimmy. I'm declaring you a Convention Refugee."

Jimmy gets refugee status.

Tears, excitement and an unbelievable wave of relief washed over Mark, Susan and Jimmy. Who could have imagined, four years earlier, when the boys first met in Uganda, that this day would ever come? For Jimmy, it meant freedom. And life.

Not long after, Jimmy was preparing to visit a school on behalf of the Ryan's Well Foundation. He was bent over a letter he was writing to the class. Susan leaned over to check his spelling and grammar. At the bottom of the page was his signature:

Jimmy Akana Hreljac

The name jumped off the page at Susan. Jimmy was home.

Ryan and Jimmy, brothers at last.

Epilogue

Around the time of the refugee hearing in October 2003, Jimmy made his first presentation about the Ryan's Well Foundation. It wasn't planned ahead of time but just happened when a Grade 4 class stopped in at Ryan and Jimmy's house as part of a field trip to Ottawa. As best he could, Jimmy told the children about how he used to get up at midnight to fetch water for his aunt before going to school.

Since then, Jimmy has become more and more involved in the Foundation. In June 2005 he made his first international trip, going to Holland with Ryan and Susan, where he met Queen Beatrix, international singer Shakira and Sir Roger Moore of James Bond fame.

He now calls Mark and Susan "Mom and Dad," and Jordan, Ryan and Keegan are his brothers. Jordan got him a part-time job pumping gas, and he was pretty popular around the gas station.

Looking to the future, Jimmy thinks he may be a teacher or a lawyer. He continued to work very hard at school, became a Canadian citizen in 2007 and graduated from university in 2012. Oh, yes — he really likes "grass" now and asks for it at every meal.

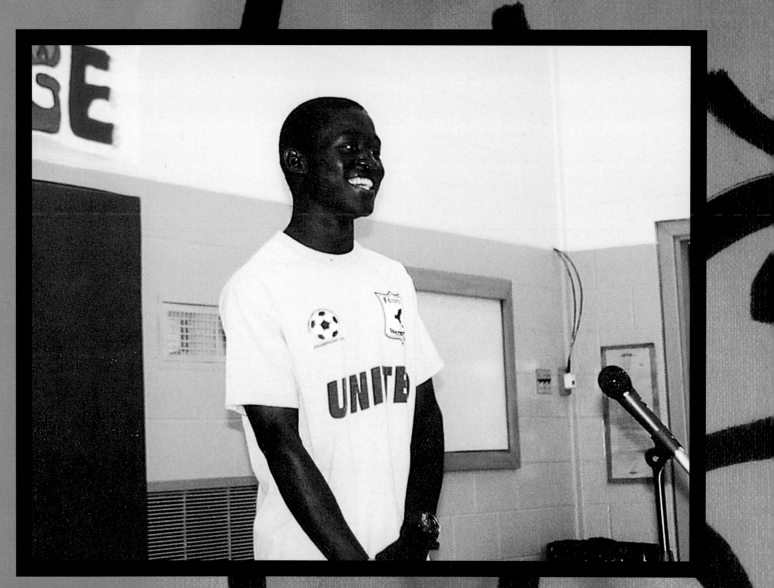

One of Jimmy's first speeches on his own was at a school in Port Hope, Ontario.

Ryan's work continues to keep him in the news. He has been on television throughout the world, including the United States, Germany, Japan, China, the Netherlands, England, Ireland, Italy, Korea, Indonesia, New Zealand, Australia and, of course, Canada. His story has been told on *The Oprah Winfrey Show* twice. Ryan met Pope John Paul II, Prince Charles, the prime minister of Canada, ocean explorer Jean-Michel Cousteau, famous scientist Jane Goodall and sports figures such as Don Cherry and Olympic gold medal winner Daniel Igali. In their own way, all of them have helped Ryan tell the story of the importance of clean water.

As for Ryan's future? Prince Charles once asked him if he'd maybe like to be a pilot some day. Ryan's not sure. He has talked about becoming a water engineer. Ryan's Well work continues to take him all over the world to conferences and other events, where he continues to speak about the importance of protecting water.

And the Ryan's Well Foundation has built more wells. As of 2013, over 725 water projects have been completed in 16 countries, bringing safe water and improved sanitation to more than 760 500 people. For more information, please go to www.ryanswell.ca.

Ryan visits a squatter's camp (a camp for people without their own homes) near Johannesburg, South Africa. The people here do not have their own well. They must wait for water to be trucked in.